Mathswork

By Steve Mills and Hilary Koll

Illustrated by Sam Lloyd

WAYLAND

Books in the series:

Mathswork 1
Mathswork 2

This book encourages children to read and helps them improve their literacy and numeracy.

- ✓ The contents page, page numbers, headings and index help locate specific pieces of information.
- ✓ The glossary reinforces alphabetic knowledge and extends vocabulary.
- ✓ The further information section suggests other books dealing with the same subject.
- ✓ Find out more about how this book is specifically relevant to the National Numeracy Strategy on page 31.

First published in 1999 by Wayland Publishers Limited, 61 Western Road, Hove, East Sussex, BN3 1JD, England

© Copyright 1999 Wayland Publishers Ltd

British Library Cataloguing in Publication Data
Mills, Steve
Mathswork 1. – (Mathswork)
I. Mathematics – Juvenile Literature
I. Title   II. Koll, Hilary
510

ISBN 0 7502 2544 0

Find Wayland on the Internet at http://www.wayland.co.uk

Typeset by Mayer Media
Printed and bound by G.Canale & C.S.p.A., Turin
Colour Separation by P&W Graphics, Singapore

contents

Des the digit detective

Des the Detective is looking for **digits**.
Digits are the numbers from 0 to 9.

- Can you see what digits Des has found?

- Which is the largest digit you can see?

- Which is the smallest?

Look around your home for digits. Make a list of the places you find them.

Des has made a list of some digits he has seen.
• How many digits has Des found?

• Which digit is not on his list?

Freddie the Frog's game

Freddie has started playing a game. The line shows the numbers from 1 to 9. He rolls a dice and jumps forward by the number the dice shows.

• Which number is he sitting on now?

These were all Freddie's throws ...

• Did he reach the finish line?

The Terrible Toad has put some signs on Freddie's game. If he lands next to a sign he must do what it says.

The signs tell him to go forward sometimes by adding on and to go backwards at other times by taking away.

• Now repeat Freddie's throws until you reach the finish. Watch out for the special signs!

Gary Green-Fingers

Gary Green-Fingers has found lots of coloured bugs on a leaf in his garden. He looks at the dots on their backs. He notices that they are all different.

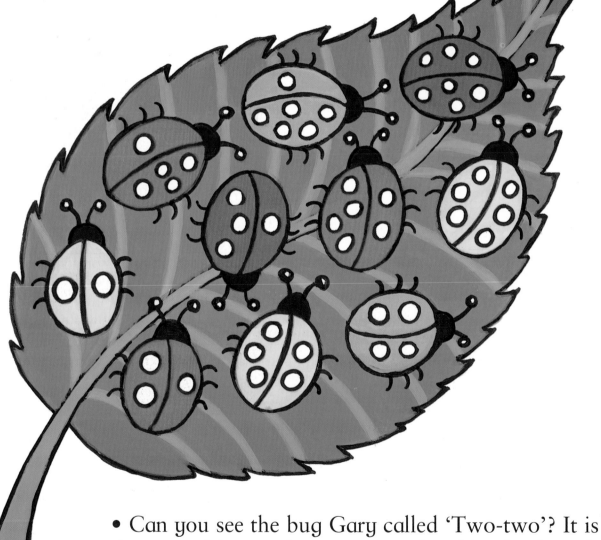

• Can you see the bug Gary called 'Two-two'? It is the one with two dots on one side of his back and two on the other.

• What do you think he called the other bugs?

Draw some bugs of your own with different numbers of dots on. Write the totals underneath. How many different types of bugs can you draw that have a total of 10?

Gary Green-Fingers made a list of all the bugs, showing how many dots each one had.

Find the **total** number of dots on each bug by adding the two numbers together.

• Do any bugs have the same total?

9

Tens jumping

Freddie the Frog and the Princess are playing a board game with two friends.

• Which numbers are the four counters on?

These are the rules of the game:
If you land on a red square you move forward 10 places. If you land on a yellow square you move forward 20 places.

Here is part of the board:

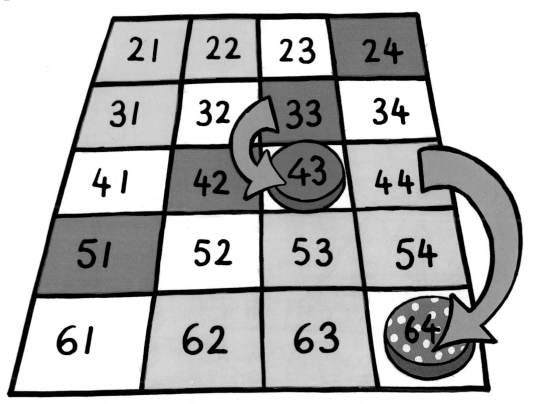

If you add 10 to any number the one's digit (units) stays the same, but the 10s digit changes.
It changes again each time you add ten.

Go back to the board game. Look at the colours of the squares:

• Where will the other two counters will move to from their place on the board?

Practise counting on in tens. Start on any number you choose and write down each number as you count in tens. Can you see the pattern?

11

King Humphrey and Queen Geraldine are in their counting house, counting out their gold and silver coins.

The King is counting his coins one by one.
The Queen is putting her coins in piles of ten and then counting them.

• Which way do you think is easier to count?
Why?

These piles of money are Queen Geraldine's coins.

- How many gold coins does Queen Geraldine have?

- How many silver coins does she have?

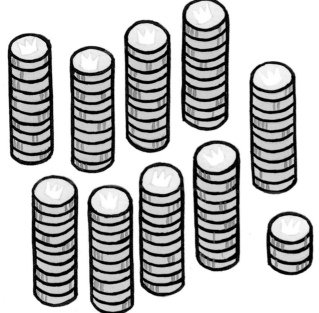 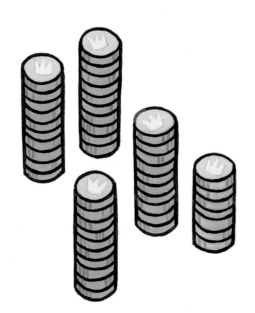

- How can you tell without counting each one?

- How many coins of each type would Queen Geraldine have left:

If she spent 10 of her gold coins;

and 21 of her silver coins?

Find the answers by taking away (subtracting).

13

Seeing double

Gruesome Gertie has made a magic potion which **doubles** things. She can turn one object into two!

If she has one bag of sweets, she can turn it into two. Here are some objects she has doubled.

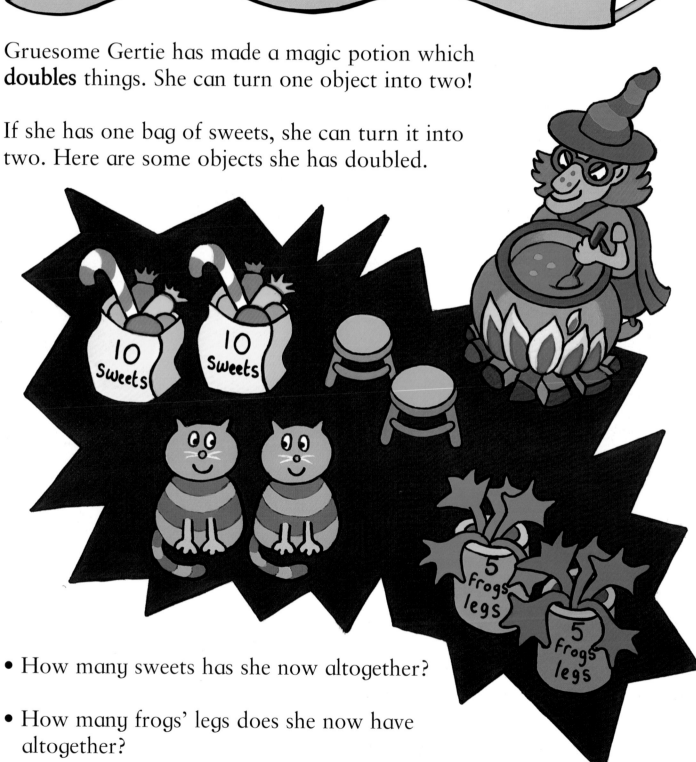

- How many sweets has she now altogether?

- How many frogs' legs does she now have altogether?

Gruesome Gertie is doubling the numbers of things she has stored on her shelves.

Find the doubles of Gertie's numbers.

- Have you noticed that when you double numbers the answers are always **even** numbers?

Do some more doubles of your own.

Make a list of things that come in twos, like ears, eyes, feet or shoes...

15

Python patterns

Here are some python **patterns**. Look at the numbers in the snakes. The numbers go up or down in 2s, 5s or 10s.

Percy
60 55 50 45 40 5 30 15 20 25

Peggy
20 16 14 12 8 6 4 2

Paul
2 4 6 8 10 14 16 18 20

Pete
40 45 50 35 30 25 20 5 10

Pat
90 100 80 70 60 40 30 20 10

- What is the name of the snake that shows numbers in the 5 times table?

- Can you work out the missing numbers of each snake?

16

These pythons have some questions, written on their bodies.

• What are the names of the pythons that have the answers to these questions? (Look at the page opposite.)

Draw an empty snake and make up some questions to match the answers to another python shown here.

Practise counting on in twos, fives or tens. Start on any number you choose. Write down each number as you go. Can you see any patterns?

The split planet

Simmy and his spaceship are about to land on a strange planet. Things on the planet are **divided** into two worlds.

On one side live things that are **symmetrical**. On the other side live things that are not symmetrical.

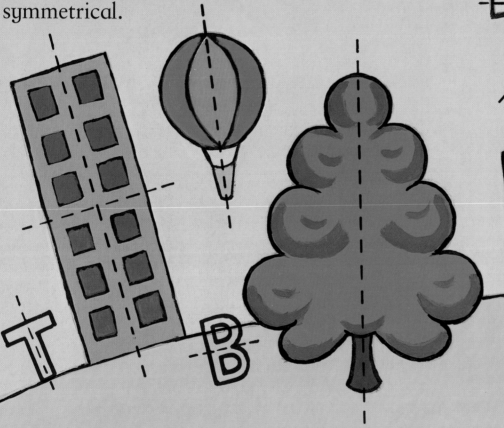

- Can you see which world is which? Shapes are symmetrical if one half is the reflection of the other half.

Use a mirror to check with, like this.

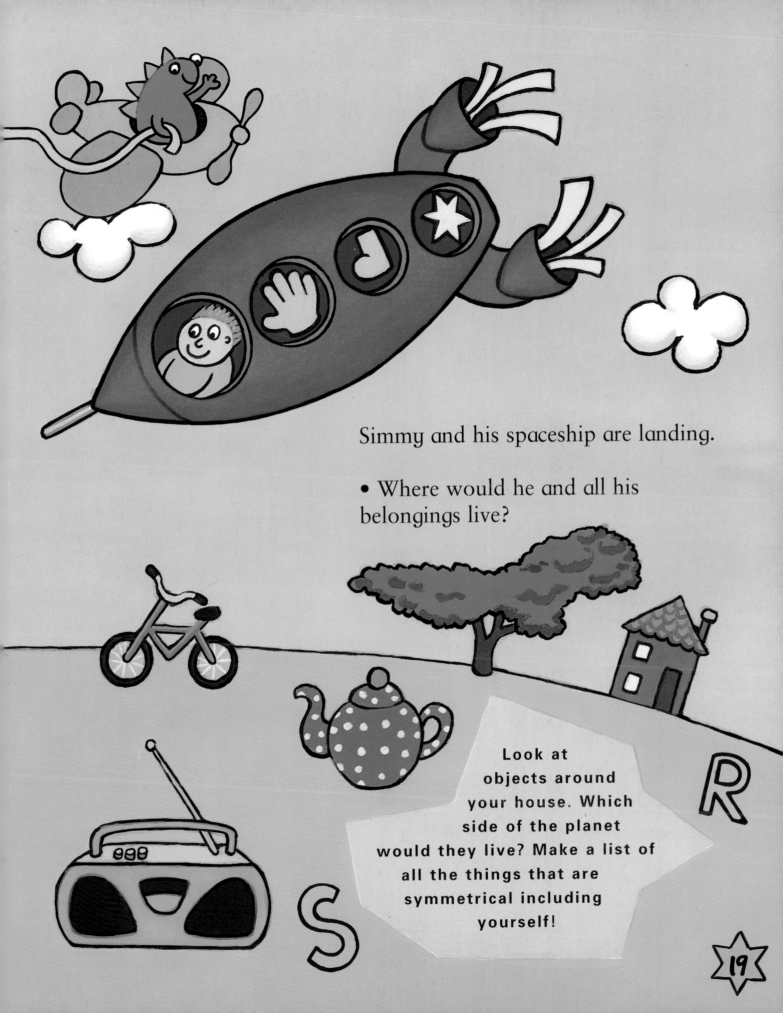

Simmy and his spaceship are landing.

• Where would he and all his belongings live?

Look at objects around your house. Which side of the planet would they live? Make a list of all the things that are symmetrical including yourself!

19

The toy cupboard

Find out the heights of some of the different toys in the toy cupboard. Help them to **measure** their heights using this ruler.

- What are the heights of all the toys, in centimetres?

- Can you put them in order, tallest first?

- How much taller is the tallest one than the shortest one?

Here is another toy, called Spaceman Sam. Using a
ruler, help Spaceman Sam to find his measurements.

- Find: the width of his hands

             the length of his legs

             the length of his arms

             the length of his feet.

Measure yourself in different ways with a ruler,
tape measure or metre stick.

- Find: the width of your hand, finger nail
             or wrist;

             the length of your arm, foot or fingers;

             your height;

             the distance around your tummy.

Travelling light

The Simpson family are going on holiday and are deciding what to pack.

Ben Simpson has put out the things that he would like to take.

1 kg

1 kg

4 kg

3 kg

4 kg

1 kg

Their ticket says they are only allowed to take 10 **kilograms** (kg) of luggage each in their bag.

1 kg

- What do all these items **weigh** together?

- Which would you choose to take?

Weigh some objects that you might take on holiday. Do they weigh more or less that 1 kg?

Ben has chosen to take items that together weigh almost 10g. He decides which final items he can pack.

• Can you choose items you think are the lightest? Put them in order, lightest first.

The topsy-turvy house

Gruesome Gertie's friend, Maisie, has built a topsy-turvy house. She has used bricks that are strange shapes. She thinks her house might fall down.

The bricks Maisie used do not have **right angles**. Right angles are sometimes called 'square corners' or 'quarter turns'. Here are some right angles.

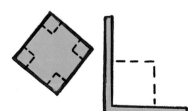

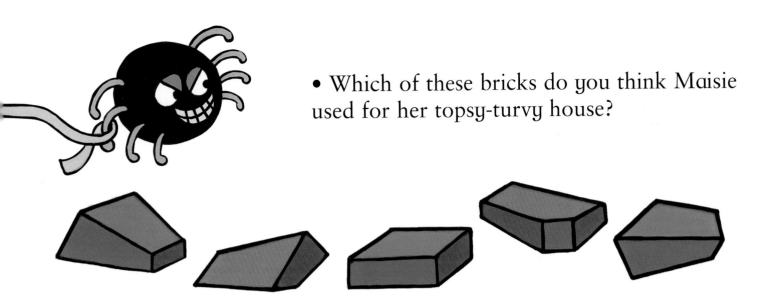

• Which of these bricks do you think Maisie used for her topsy-turvy house?

Maisie decides to build a new house with right-angled bricks.

Look around your home for right angles. Look at windows, pictures, cupboards and doors.

• Can you find all the right angles in her new house?

25

Adventure playground

Here is the adventure playground.
There are lots of different shapes in this picture.

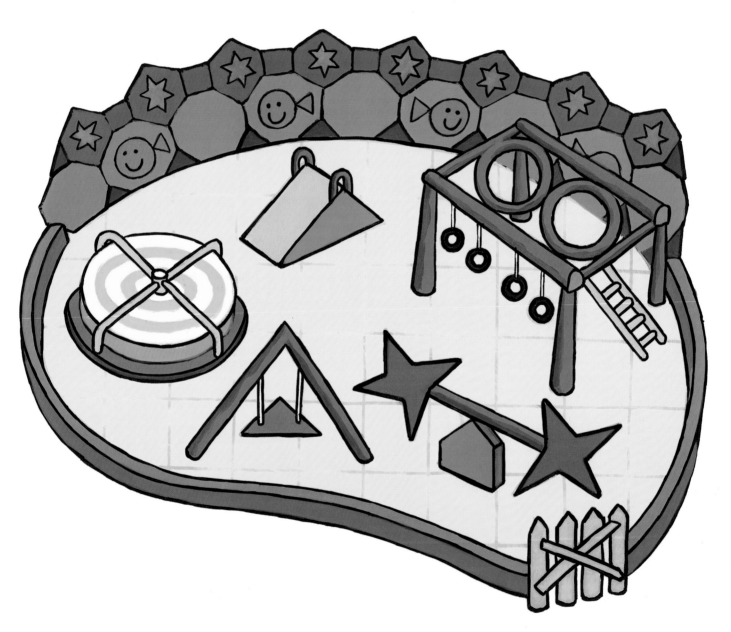

• How many different shapes can you see?

26

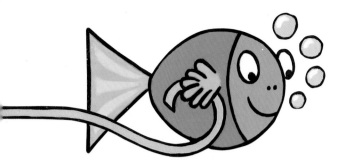

Draw a picture of your own, using different shapes. Make a key to show the shapes you have used.

• Do you know the names of the shapes?

Look at this key to help you.

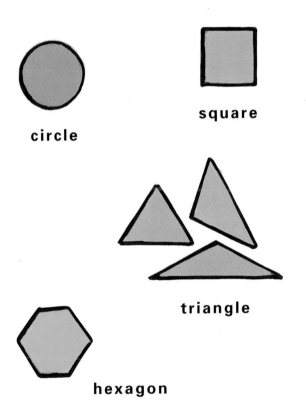

circle

square

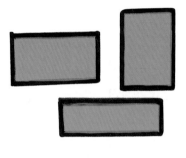

rectangle

triangle

pentagon

hexagon

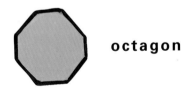

octagon

Look at the adventure playground.

What shapes make up:

• the swing?   • the slide?   • the see-saw?

• the roundabout?   • the mural?   • the climbing frame?

27

What's the time Mr Wolf?

Mr Wolf is waiting for Little Red Riding Hood inside her Granny's house. He knows she will be arriving at 3 o'clock.

There are many different types of clocks in Granny's house and all the clocks are set at different times.

• Do any of the clocks show 3 o'clock?

• Can you find the clock that is set at half past four?

• Or the clock showing five to six?

• What times do the other clocks show?

29

Glossary

Digits These are the ten symbols we use to write numbers 0, 1, 2, 3, 4, 5, 6, 7, 8, 9. The word 'figure' can also be used.

Divided When something is cut into equal parts.

Double When we double a number we find the answer to twice the original number, eg. double 5 is 10.

Even All numbers are either odd or even. An even number can be divided into two whole, equal parts.

Kilogram A unit of weight made up of one thousand grams.

Measure To find out the size of something.

Patterns Designs that have been created.

Right angle This is a quarter of a complete turn.

Symmetrical A name given to a shape if the two halves of a shape are a reflection of each other. The line which separates them is called a 'line of symmetry'.

Total The total is the answer we get by adding up a set of numbers. The word 'sum' can also be used.

Weigh To find out how heavy something is.

Notes for Adults

Maths is one of the most important subjects to gain a solid understanding of at a young age. This book can be used in school or at home and has been designed to enable young children to feel confident in working with numbers, patterns and shapes that form the basis of future work.

The book consists of a series of fun situations, activities and games which build a framework of facts, skills and concepts for Number and Shape work at Key Stage 1. There are also ideas for extension work on each page.

Mathswork 1 meets the main requirements of Key Stage 1 Number and Shape, Space and Measures at Levels 1-3.

Pupils at Key Stage 1 should be able to:
- develop flexible methods of working with number
- use a variety of practical resources and contexts
- use patterns to develop ideas of regularity and sequencing
- develop a variety of methods for addition and subtraction
- gain a feel for the approximate size of a number
- use purposeful contexts for measuring
- describe and discuss shapes and patterns that can be seen or visualized
- understand and recognize right angles
- understand and use appropriate measures

This book meets objectives of the National Numeracy Strategy's Framework for Teaching in the following areas:

✓ Numbers and the number system.

✓ Calculations.

✓ Handling data.

✓ Measures, shape and space.

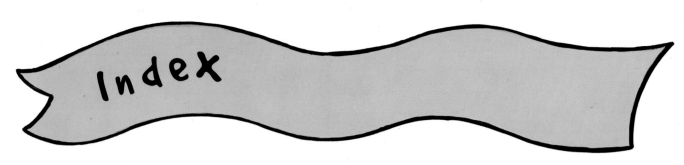

Index

Books to read

Mathswork 2 by Steve Mills and Hilary Koll (Wayland, 1999)

Holiday (Letts, 1998)

Maths Detectives series (Ladybird, 1998)

Basic Skills (Letts, 1998)